W9-CZW-652

THOMAS CRANE PUBLIC LIBRARY
QUINCY MASS
CITY APPROPRIATION

NOV -- 2011

GIGANTIC LENGTHS AND OTHER VAST MEGASTRUCTURES

Ian Graham

QEB Publishing

Created for QED Publishing by Tall Tree Ltd
www.talltreebooks.co.uk
Editor: Rob Colson
Designers: Malcolm Parchment and Jonathan Vipond
Illustrations: Apple Illustration and Caroline Watson

Copyright © QEB Publishing, Inc. 2011

Published in the United States by
QEB Publishing, Inc.
3 Wrigley, Suite A
Irvine, CA 92618

www.qed-publishing.co.uk

All rights reserved. No part of this publication may be reproduced,
stored in a retrieval system, or transmitted in any form or by any means,
electronic, mechanical, photocopying, recording, or otherwise, without
the prior permission of the publisher, nor be otherwise circulated in any
form of binding or cover other than that in which it is published and
without a similar condition being imposed on the subsequent purchaser.

A CIP record for this book is available from the
Library of Congress.

ISBN 978 1 60992 097 5

Printed in China

Picture credits
(t=top, b=bottom, l=left, r=right, c=centre)
12-13 David Lee Photography; 13 Lee Jackson; 14 BLS AG; 24-25 Markuskun; 30-31 Femern
AS **Alamy** 7t Thomas Jackson; 14-15 qaphotos.com; 15 qaphotos.com; 21 Dominic Twist;
25 David R. Frazier Photolibrary, Inc.; **Corbis** 5b Mark Thiessen/National Geographic
Society; 8 Imaginechina; 9t Frederic Stevens/epa; 30 Jacques Langevin/Sygma;
20-21 Andrew Kendrick/US Coast Guard; 22-23 Stringer/China/Reuters; 29 Bettmann;
30 Jacques Langevin/Sygma; **Dreamstime** 7b Redeyed; **Getty images** 12 Cleland
Rimmer/Fox Photos; 20b AFP; 26 Hulton Archive; **Photolibrary** 9b Thomas Frey;
Shutterstock 4-5 Jarno Gonzalez Zarraonandia; 5t Francisco Caravana 6-7 Laitr Keiows;
10-11 Manamana; 11t SVLuma; 11b clearviewstock; 16-17 Brendan Howard; 18-19 Antony
McAulay; 19l E. Petersen; 23t Luis Santos; 26-27 Rafael Ramirez Lee; 27 Shutterstock;
28-29 r.nagy;

Words in **bold** are explained in the Glossary on page 32.

Contents

Over and under

Bridges and tunnels have been built since ancient times, but today they are bigger and longer than ever. These amazing engineering projects enable cars and other vehicles to take a more direct route across wide stretches of water or through the middle of mountains.

Building bridges

Bridges have developed from the simple ropes and vines that spanned rivers in prehistoric times to today's graceful steel and concrete structures that seem to defy gravity. The giant bridges built today are so long that they have to be shaped to fit the curve of the Earth's surface.

Tunnels

While bridges stand tall in the open for everyone to see, tunnels are hidden under the ground. The longest tunnels carry water into cities from distant **reservoirs**, but the most impressive tunnels are those through which we can travel: road and railroad tunnels. The longest transport tunnel in use today is the Seikan Tunnel. This 34-mile (54-kilometer) railroad tunnel links the Japanese islands of Honshu and Hokkaido under the sea.

MEGA FACTS

The 86-mile-long (137 kilometer) Delaware Aqueduct is the world's longest tunnel. It is part of a network that supplies New York City with water.

▲ The Bosphorus Bridge is a suspension bridge in Istanbul, Turkey. It links the continents of Europe and Asia.

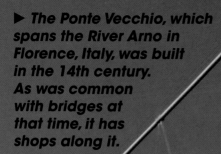

► *The Ponte Vecchio, which spans the River Arno in Florence, Italy, was built in the 14th century. As was common with bridges at that time, it has shops along it.*

Particle smasher

There is a tunnel 574 feet (175 meters) under the border between France and Switzerland that does not lead anywhere. It goes round in a circle, 17 miles (27 kilometers) in circumference. The tunnel was built in the 1980s to house a scientific instrument called the Large Electron–Positron Collider. Subatomic particles were fired through a pipe inside the 12.5-foot-wide (4 meter) tunnel, and scientists studied what happened when they collided. Today, there is a new scientific instrument, the Large Hadron Collider, in the tunnel.

▲ *Particles hurtle around the Large Hadron Collider at close to the speed of light.*

▶ The Akashi Kaikyo Bridge in Japan is stiffened by metal beams linked together in triangles, creating a very strong structure.

Building long

Bridge and tunnel designers and engineers have to overcome several problems. For example, bridges have to cope with every type of weather, from blistering heat to freezing cold. Tunnels have to resist the crushing weight of the ground above them.

Stretching bridges

Materials grow bigger when they heat up. On a hot day, a bridge expands and becomes longer. Joints, called expansion joints, are built into the **roadway** of a bridge. They let the roadway grow longer without causing any damage. Arch-shaped bridges made from steel **girders** expand in length and height when they heat up. Hinges are built into the arch to let it expand.

MEGA FACTS

On a hot day, the steel arch of Sydney Harbour Bridge can expand and rise by up to 7 inches (18 centimeters). Hinges at each end of the bridge let it rise and fall safely.

Resisting weight

When a long tunnel is dug, the weight of the ground above it will eventually squash it flat unless the tunnelers strengthen it. To keep a new tunnel in the right shape, it is lined with a strong, thick layer of **reinforced concrete**. Deep tunnels are usually circular as this shape is very strong.

▲ *Pedestrians walk across the bridge when the "eye" is closed.*

▲ *The walkway tilts up to allow ships to pass underneath the bridge.*

Bridges are often built over busy shipping lanes. Low bridges often have sections that open to let boats through. The Gateshead Millennium Bridge over the Tyne River in England, UK makes room for boats in an unusual way: the ends of the curved bridge stay attached to the river's banks while the rest of the bridge tilts up. Because of the way it opens, it is known as the "Blinking Eye Bridge."

How are they built?

The world's longest bridges and tunnels are huge projects. Whether engineers are planning to build a bridge or a tunnel, the first thing they do is find out what the ground is like. They bore holes in it and take samples to see what it is made of and how strong it is. Because bridges are very heavy, they must stand on solid rock, so bridge builders also need to know how far the bedrock is below the surface.

Bridge-building

Building a bridge begins with the construction of **piers**, the supports that hold up the bridge. Depending on what type of bridge it is, tall towers might have to be built on top of some of the piers to support cables that hold up the bridge's **deck**. A suspension bridge's cables are fixed at each end of the bridge to massive concrete blocks called **anchorages**. Next, the bridge's roadway, or deck, is lifted into position, section by section. A floating crane does this job for a low bridge over water, but the biggest bridges are too high for most floating cranes. For these bridges, hooks are lowered from the bridge itself to lift the bridge sections from barges in the water below.

▶ Workers finish building the deck of the Hangzhou Bay Bridge, the world's longest sea bridge, near Shanghai, China, in 2007.

► *The Millau Viaduct in France was built in a different way from most bridges. Half of the deck was built at each end of the bridge. Then the two halves were slid out onto the tops of supporting towers until they met in the middle.*

Tunneling

Tunnelers need to know what sort of rock they are dealing with. Once they know, they can decide how to build the tunnel. One way is to use a **tunnel boring machine (TBM)**, which goes through the ground like a huge earthworm. A toothed disc, called the cutter head, on the front of a TBM rotates slowly, grinding away the rock. If the rocks are too hard for a TBM to cut, Tunnelers use explosives instead. The rock shattered by the explosions is hauled out of the tunnel and the walls are lined with concrete.

▼ *A giant TBM is prepared for digging. Its service train stretches behind it.*

MEGA FACTS

Each of the concrete anchorages at the ends of the Golden Gate Bridge, San Fransisco, weighs more than 54,000 tons (54,000 tonnes)—that is heavier than a battleship.

9

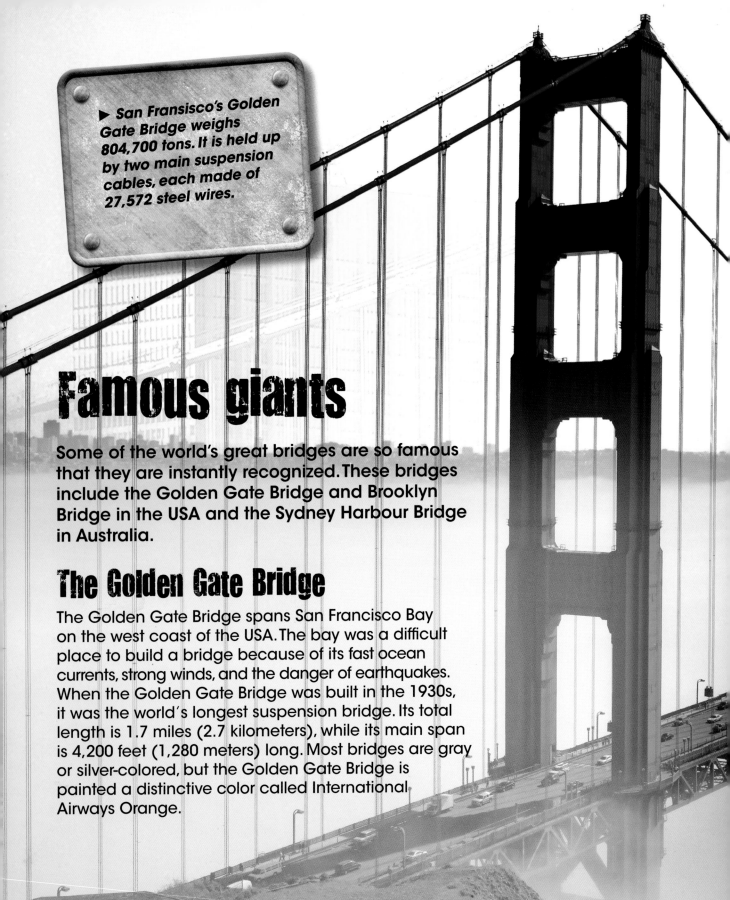

▶ San Fransisco's Golden Gate Bridge weighs 804,700 tons. It is held up by two main suspension cables, each made of 27,572 steel wires.

Famous giants

Some of the world's great bridges are so famous that they are instantly recognized. These bridges include the Golden Gate Bridge and Brooklyn Bridge in the USA and the Sydney Harbour Bridge in Australia.

The Golden Gate Bridge

The Golden Gate Bridge spans San Francisco Bay on the west coast of the USA. The bay was a difficult place to build a bridge because of its fast ocean currents, strong winds, and the danger of earthquakes. When the Golden Gate Bridge was built in the 1930s, it was the world's longest suspension bridge. Its total length is 1.7 miles (2.7 kilometers), while its main span is 4,200 feet (1,280 meters) long. Most bridges are gray or silver-colored, but the Golden Gate Bridge is painted a distinctive color called International Airways Orange.

The Brooklyn Bridge

The Brooklyn Bridge links Brooklyn with Manhattan across New York City's East River. It was built between 1869 and 1883. The Brooklyn Bridge is a suspension bridge supported by two enormous **masonry** towers 1,595 feet (486 meters) apart. When the bridge opened, it carried a pair of railroad tracks with roads on each side and a walkway for pedestrians. The railroad tracks were removed in 1944.

◄ *The Brooklyn Bridge was the first to have suspension cables made of steel. Until then, cables were made of iron.*

Sydney Harbour Bridge

Australia's Sydney Harbour Bridge is the world's biggest steel arch bridge. The two halves of the arch were built out from opposite sides of the harbor until they met in the middle. Then the deck was hung from the arch. The whole bridge is held together by six million **rivets**, which were all driven into place by hand. The bridge carries eight vehicle lanes, two railroad tracks, a **footway**, and a cycle lane.

◄ *The arch of the Sydney Harbour Bridge is 1,650 feet (503 meters) long and rises to a height of 440 feet (134 meters).*

11

There had been plans for a bridge or tunnel across the estuary of the Humber River in northeast England, UK, since the 1870s, but work on the project did not finally begin until 1959. The first decision to be made was whether to build a bridge or a tunnel. A bridge was chosen because geologists found that the ground under the river was not suitable for tunneling.

Spanning the estuary

The shifting sands in the estuary meant that the deep-water channel used by ships kept moving. Because of this, the bridge could not rest on a series of piers across the river, so it was decided to build a suspension bridge. Construction work on the bridge began in 1973. A pier was built at each side of the river and a concrete tower was built on top of each pier. The towers are 4,626 feet (1,410 meters) apart and the total length of the bridge is 7,218 feet (2,200 meters). The suspension cables were strung between massive concrete anchorages at each end of the bridge.

◄ *The bridge's towers are so tall that their tops sometimes peek out above the low clouds that settle over the river.*

◄ *The supporting tower on the north bank of the river starts to take shape one year into the bridge's construction.*

The Humber Bridge

length: 7,220 feet (2,200 m)

◀ *When the Humber Bridge opened in 1981, it was the world's longest single-span suspension bridge. It held the record until 1998, when it was overtaken by Japan's Akashi Kaikyo Bridge.*

Laying the deck

The deck was built in steel sections 72 feet (22 meters) across—wide enough for four lanes of traffic. A 10-feet (3-meter) strip added to each side of the deck carries cycle tracks and footways. The deck was hoisted into position, section by section, and hung from the cables. bridge was completed in 1981.

MEGA FACTS

Because of the curvature of the Earth's surface, the Humber Bridge's towers are 1.4 inches (36 millimeters) further apart at the top than at the bottom.

The longest tunnels

Road and rail tunnels can cut hours off journey times by providing more direct routes through mountains. The longest tunnels include the Guadarrama Railway Tunnel in Spain and the Lötschberg Base Tunnel in Switzerland.

The train in Spain

In 2007, a new railroad tunnel through the Guadarrama Mountains in Spain opened. The Guadarrama Railway Tunnel was Europe's fourth-longest rail tunnel. It was built to carry high-speed trains that run at up to 190 miles per hour. (300 kilometers per hour) The twin-bore tunnel was carved out of the rock by four tunnel boring machines (TBMs). Two machines set out from the ends of the two tunnels towards each other. They were guided so accurately that they were only 4 inches (10 centimeters) out of line when they met. The TBMs bored two tunnels 31 feet (9.5 meters) across. The two tunnels are connected every 820 feet (250 meters) by cross-tunnels.

Through the Alps

▲ The two tubes of the tunnel are connected to each other every 1,092 feet (333 meters), so each tunnel can be used as an emergency escape route for the other tunnel.

The Alps mountain range forms a natural barrier between Italy and the rest of Europe. Since the 1870s, more than a dozen tunnels have been dug through the mountains. In 2007, the Lötschberg Base Tunnel opened, cutting the journey time between Germany and Italy by a third. The ground was very difficult to cut through because it was made of hard rock. Some of the tunnel could be dug by TBMs, but most of it had to be blasted out with explosives.

► Machines called roadheaders are used to dig tunnels that are too small and short for TBMs.

◄ Because TBMs are so big, they are usually assembled and taken apart deep underground.

MEGA FACTS

When it was completed in October 2010, the 35-mile-long (56 kilometer) Gotthard Base Tunnel in the Alps became the world's longest railroad tunnel.

MEGA FACTS

During construction of the Øresund Link, workers found 16 unexploded bombs on the seabed. The bombs had been dropped during World War II (1939–45).

Peberholm Island

The bridge and tunnel meet at an artificial island called Peberholm. It was made from sand, stone, and mud **dredged** from the seabed. More than to 265 million cubic feet (7.5 million cubic meters) of seabed had to be dug up. That is enough to fill 3,000 Olympic-size swimming pools.

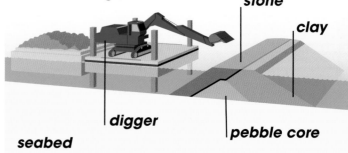

stone

clay

digger

pebble core

seabed

▲ The dyke (wall) built around Peberholm Island was covered with stone to protect it from damage caused by waves.

double-decker bridge carries cars (above) and trains (below)

In 1991, the governments of Sweden and Denmark agreed to build a link between their two countries. It was to cross a stretch of water called the Øresund **Strait**, connecting the Danish capital Copenhagen to the Swedish city of Malmö. The link was divided into two parts—a bridge and a tunnel. The tunnel was chosen for the Danish side of the crossing because a bridge with tall towers could have been a danger to low-flying aircraft near Copenhagen Airport.

Cable-stayed bridge

The Øresund Bridge stands on a line of concrete piers 460 feet (140 meters) apart. Once the piers were built, the bridge deck was lifted into position on top of them. Each 460-foot (140-meter) section of the deck weighed 6,500 tons (6,500 tonnes). The bridge has two decks, one above the other. Road traffic uses the upper deck and trains use the lower deck. The decks rise gently from each end to a height of 180 feet (55 meters) in the middle. There are no piers underneath the middle section so that ships can sail under it. This part of the bridge is held up by cables hanging from two tall towers called pylons. This is an example of a cable-stayed bridge.

▼ The Øresund Bridge has the world's longest cable-stayed main span at 3,583 feet (1,092 meters).

The Øresund Link

total length: 10.3 miles (16.4 km) bridge length

Short and long

Bridges can be built using many different techniques depending on the length of the gap to be spanned and the kind of ground on which the bridge stands. Short bridges just a few feet (meters) long are usually built as beam bridges. Most of the longest bridges, some of them several miles (kilometers) long, are suspension bridges.

Beam

The simplest type of bridge is a beam bridge—a beam supported at each end. A tree trunk laid across a stream is a beam bridge, so beam bridges were probably the first bridges ever built. They are still used for bridging narrow gaps.

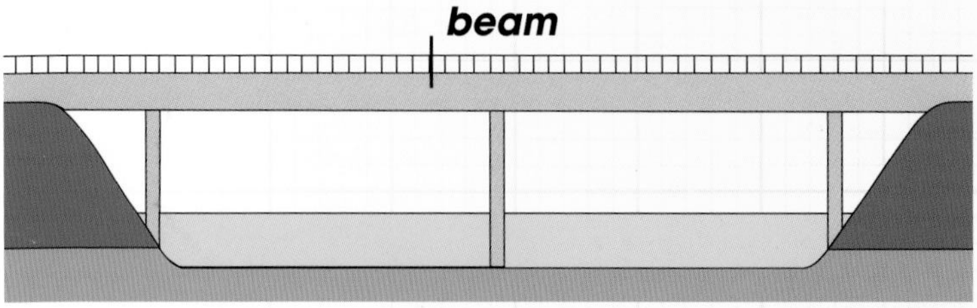

beam

Arch

An arch is a curved structure that spans a gap. It can support more weight than a beam bridge. The weight of an arch bridge tries to push the ends of the bridge apart. Massive blocks called **abutments** hold them in place.

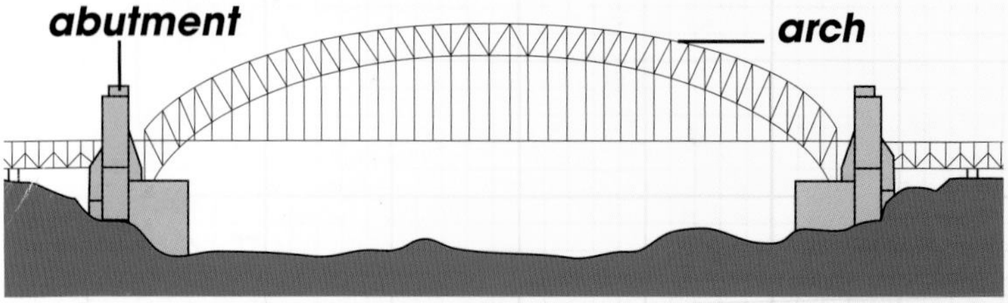

abutment ——— *arch*

Cantilever

A **cantilever** is a beam held up at one end only, like a shelf. One way to build a cantilever bridge is to build decks out from both sides of a tower so that they balance each other. The two parts of the deck are the cantilevers.

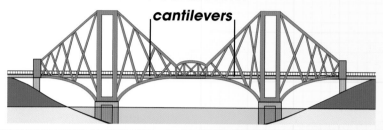
cantilevers

Suspension

In a suspension bridge, two cables run from one end of the bridge to the other. They pass over the tops of tall towers. Thinner cables, called **hangers**, hang from the suspension cables.

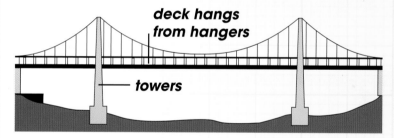
deck hangs from hangers

towers

Cable-stayed

A cable-stayed bridge has a deck held up by cables, but unlike a suspension bridge there are no suspension cables running the length of the bridge. Instead, the deck hangs from cables attached to the bridge's towers.

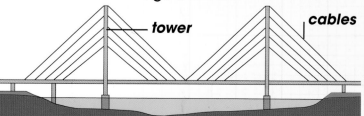
tower

cables

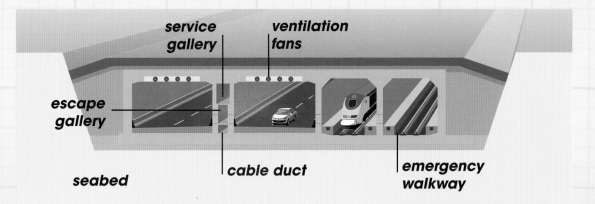

service gallery

ventilation fans

escape gallery

seabed

cable duct

emergency walkway

▲ The tunnel carries two two-lane roadways and two railroad tracks inside four side-by-side galleries. In case of emergencies, there is an escape tunnel between the railroad and walkways alongside the railroad tracks.

Royal opening

The first vehicle drove through the tunnel in March 1999. In 2000, Queen Margrethe II of Denmark and King Carl XVI Gustaf of Sweden opened the completed bridge–tunnel link to the public. Every year, more than 25 million people cross the Øresund Link, including 15 million traveling by car and more than 10 million by train. In December 2010, the City Tunnel, a 11-mile (17-kilometer) rail link from the Øresund Link to Malmö Central Station, was opened. It carries passengers under the streets of Malmö to the center of the city.

pylons

◄ *The tunnel sits in a trench dug into the seabed. In total, it weighs 1.1 million tons (1.1 million tonnes), equivalent to the weight of 10 large cruise ships.*

Tunnel to Denmark

The tunnel was made in sections in a factory built specially for the job. The tunnel sections were made from concrete. Each section was enormous, measuring 577 feet (176 meters) long, 30 feet (9 meters) high, and 131 feet (40 meters) wide, and weighing 55,000 tons (55,000 tonnes). One by one, 20 of these sections were floated out to the right position and then lowered from barges into a trench dug in the seabed. When they were in position, they were connected. Then the tunnel was covered with mud and clay from the seabed to weigh it down and protect it from being hit by a ship or a ship's anchor.

location: Øresund Strait between Denmark and Sweden

The hazard factor

Bridges and tunnels face a number of **hazards,** from traffic accidents to extreme weather. They are constantly monitored to check for any damage or decay and to make sure they remain safe.

Cold comfort

Icy roads are often treated with salt to melt the ice. The salty water this produces can sink down into a bridge's concrete roadway and rust the steel bars inside the concrete. Steel expands when it rusts. If the steel bars inside concrete rust, they expand and crack the concrete.

MEGA FACTS

Pigeons can pose a serious danger to bridges. They like to perch on the cables and beams, and their droppings eat into the steel and weaken it.

Forces of nature

Deep underground, tunnels are protected from the storms that can damage bridges, but they may be destroyed by earthquakes that move the ground. Tunnels are carefully checked for damage after every quake.

▲ When an earthquake shook Sweden on December 16, 2008, technicians checked the Drogden Tunnel to make sure it had not been damaged. They did this by measuring the distance between fixed points to check that they had not moved.

► The I-10 Bridge in Florida was damaged by Hurricane Ivan in 2004. More than 100 sections were pushed out of place or collapsed altogether.

Falling ice

Cold weather can produce other dangers to traffic on a bridge. Ice can build up on the bridge's cables and **gantries** until chunks big enough to smash a car windshield crash to the ground. Bridges may have to close if falling ice makes them too dangerous to cross.

Pinging cables

Some suspension bridges suffer from a problem that weakens their suspension cables. If moisture gets in between the steel wires that make up the massive cables, the wires rust. Within a few years, they start breaking. If this continues unchecked, year after year, the bridge will eventually become dangerously weak. Microphones attached to the cables pick up the pinging sounds made by the breaking wires. One way to stop the problem getting any worse is to pump dry air through the cables to drive out the moisture. This process is called dehumidification.

▼ *The cables that hold up the Forth Road Bridge in Scotland, UK, wrap around holders, called yokes, in concrete chambers. The cables are regularly inspected for damage.*

Monster spans

China's Hangzhou Bay Bridge and Portugal's Vasco da Gama Bridge are among the world's longest bridges. The Hangzhou Bay Bridge is the world's longest bridge over sea, while the Vasco da Gama Bridge is Europe's longest bridge.

China's record-breaker

The 23-mile-long (36 kilometer) Hangzhou Bay Bridge links China's most populous city, Shanghai, with the city of Ningbo. The bridge crosses Hangzhou Bay, part of the East China Sea, an area with strong currents that is regularly battered by tropical storms. Most of the bridge is made of short spans sitting on top of piers anchored to the seabed, but two parts of the bridge are higher than the rest and held up by cables hanging from towers. These cable-stayed spans have no supports below the deck, which means that ships can sail underneath them.

MEGA FACTS

Nearly 600 experts worked for nine years on the design of the Hangzhou Bay Bridge, because it was to be built in such a difficult place for a bridge.

▲ The Hangzhou Bay Bridge carries a six-lane highway across the sea. It opened in 2008 and is designed to last for 100 years.

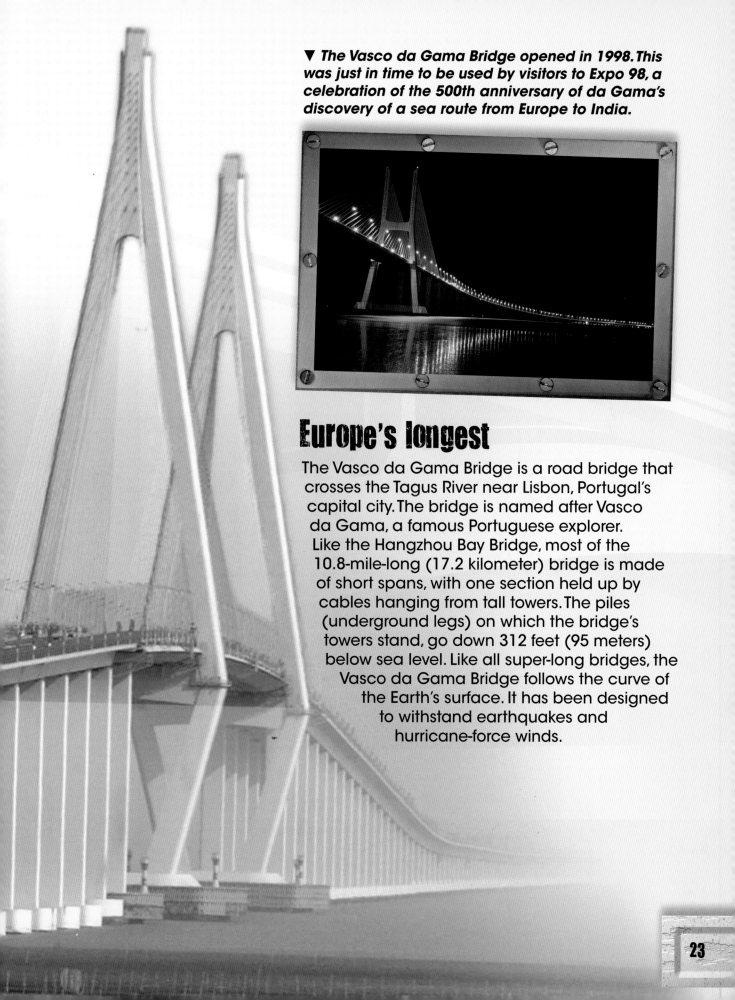

▼ *The Vasco da Gama Bridge opened in 1998. This was just in time to be used by visitors to Expo 98, a celebration of the 500th anniversary of da Gama's discovery of a sea route from Europe to India.*

Europe's longest

The Vasco da Gama Bridge is a road bridge that crosses the Tagus River near Lisbon, Portugal's capital city. The bridge is named after Vasco da Gama, a famous Portuguese explorer. Like the Hangzhou Bay Bridge, most of the 10.8-mile-long (17.2 kilometer) bridge is made of short spans, with one section held up by cables hanging from tall towers. The piles (underground legs) on which the bridge's towers stand, go down 312 feet (95 meters) below sea level. Like all super-long bridges, the Vasco da Gama Bridge follows the curve of the Earth's surface. It has been designed to withstand earthquakes and hurricane-force winds.

The Lake Pontchartrain Causeway in Louisiana, is the world's longest bridge over water. From end to end, it measures 24 miles (38.4 kilometers). It is so long that, because of the curved shape of the Earth's surface, someone standing at one end of the bridge cannot see the other end. The causeway spans Lake Pontchartrain, the second-biggest saltwater lake in the USA. The city of New Orleans lies on the lake's south shore.

Twin bridges

The causeway is actually two bridges side by side. The first bridge was finished in 1956. It proved so popular that within 10 years, more than 3,000 vehicles were using it every day. A second bridge was built alongside. It opened in 1969. The bridges are linked together at seven points, so that traffic can cross from one bridge to the other in an emergency. There are also drawbridges, called **bascules**, that open to let boats thorugh.

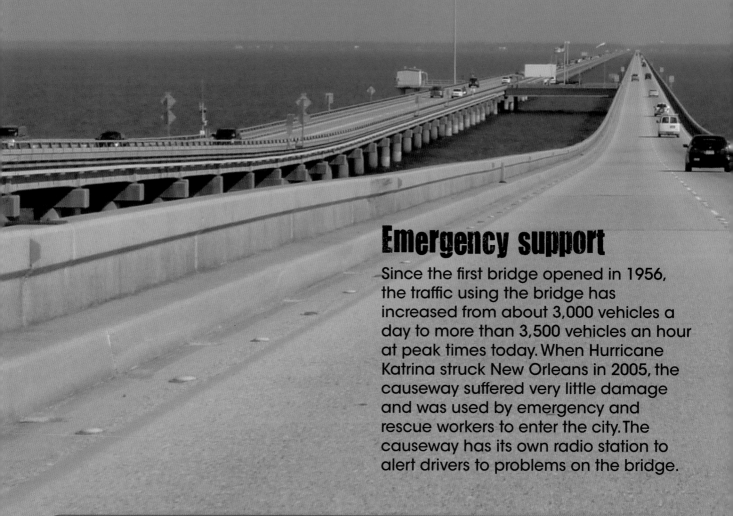

Emergency support

Since the first bridge opened in 1956, the traffic using the bridge has increased from about 3,000 vehicles a day to more than 3,500 vehicles an hour at peak times today. When Hurricane Katrina struck New Orleans in 2005, the causeway suffered very little damage and was used by emergency and rescue workers to enter the city. The causeway has its own radio station to alert drivers to problems on the bridge.

Lake Pontchartrain Causeway

length: 24 miles (38.4 km)

◀ A bascule opens to let boats through. Fenders protect the bridge from bumps by boats as they pass through. A radar system alerts officials if a boat comes within 1 mile (1.6 kilometers) of the bridge.

▼ The twin spans of the Lake Pontchartrain Causeway disappear over the horizon. Driving at 70 miles (115 kilometers) per hour, it takes more than 20 minutes to cross the bridge.

MEGA FACTS

The Lake Pontchartrain Causeway is so long that it spans one-thousandth of the Earth's circumference.

Subways

Railroad systems that snake through a network of underground tunnels are called subways. They can move passengers across a busy city very quickly because the trains are not held up by heavy traffic or bad weather on the surface.

6 CARS - BOARD
PLATFORM 1

The first subway tunnels were built using the "cut and cover" method. First, a large trench was dug down the middle of a street. Then the street was rebuilt on top of the tunnel. Today, subway tunnels may be more than 200 feet (60 meters) below the surface, and they are usually dug using tunnel boring machines (TBMs).

New York Subway

TBMs have become much more powerful over the years. The machine that is digging the new Second Avenue line in New York City is as powerful as 12 jumbo jets and can grind its way through 60 feet (18 meters) of rock a day. It was manufactured in about 1980 and has been used on at least four other projects. This latest subway line is due to open in 2016.

▲ *This TBM was used during the construction of subway lines in New York City in the 1930s.*

Going electric

London was the first city in the world to have an underground railroad. The first section, the Metropolitan line, opened in 1863. Today, there are 11 lines with routes covering more than 250 miles (400 kilometers). The Northern line is the deepest line: in places it is 230 feet (70 meters) below ground. Electric trains were used from the beginning because they did not produce choking fumes like steam engines did.

▶ Flooding is a problem in subway networks. More than 8 million gallons of water a day are pumped out of the London Underground.

▲ The subway system for San Francisco, known as the BART, has a WiFi system that allows passengers to access the Internet from the trains.

27

Failures and accidents

Engineers understand the forces that act on tunnels and bridges, but these enormous structures can sometimes surprise them. Accidents can happen to even the best-designed structures. Bridge designers try to make their bridges flexible enough to soak up small movements caused by strong winds and traffic, but stiff enough to stand safely for many years.

The Wobbly Bridge

When the Millennium Bridge, a footbridge across the River Thames in London, UK, opened in 2000, it swayed so much that it was nicknamed the "Wobbly Bridge." The problem was caused by something called synchronous lateral excitation. When people walked on the bridge, their footsteps made it sway a little from side to side. As soon as people felt this movement, they could not help walking in time with it, which made the swaying even worse. The bridge was closed while devices called dampers were fitted to fix the swaying.

▶ *The cables that hold up London's Millennium Bridge run along the sides rather than hanging above it.*

In 1879, part of an iron railroad bridge across the Tay River in Scotland collapsed in a storm. A passenger train crossing the bridge fell into the river.

Tunnel fires

Fires are a serious danger in tunnels. In 1999, a truck caught fire in the Mont Blanc Tunnel, which passes under Mont Blanc, Western Europe's highest mountain. The fire spread through the tunnel so fast that 39 people died. Over the next three years, shelters, fire-resistant wall coverings, smoke extractors, heat sensors, and a fire station were built to make the tunnel safer.

Galloping Gertie

When a suspension bridge across the Tacoma Narrows Strait in Washington state, opened on July 1, 1940, it moved about so much in the wind that it was nicknamed "Galloping Gertie." Four months later, the bridge twisted to and fro so violently that it broke up. The collapse was caused by something called aeroelastic flutter. When the bridge started moving in the wind, its bendiness let it twist back and forth until it shook itself to bits.

◀ *The roadway of the Tacoma Narrows Bridge hangs in shreds. A wind of only 40 miles (64 kilometers) per hour made the bridge twist so much that it tore itself apart.*

Future bridges and tunnels

The longest bridges and tunnels in use today are marvels of engineering, but even longer transport links are being planned. Some of these are bridges that will smash the records set by today's bridges. Many of the world's new bridges will be built in East Asia. In particular, China is now a wealthy country that wants to link its big cities to make it easier for businesses to move people, materials, and products between the cities and ports.

Bering Bridge

One of the most daring plans is for a bridge to link Russia and the USA across the Bering Strait. The bridge could carry a roadway, rail tracks, and pipelines for oil and natural gas. Three bridges will be needed to span the strait—one from Russia to the Diomede Islands, one between the islands, and a third from the islands to Alaska. Two of the three bridges will have to be longer than China's Hangzhou Bay Bridge—the longest sea bridge in the world today.

▲ *A bridge across the Bering Strait would be 55 miles long in total, passing over the Diomede Islands that lie halfway across the strait.*

Crossing the Pearl River

The Hong Kong–Zhuhai–Macao Bridge in China will be 30 miles (50 kilometers) long, with 22 miles (35 kilometers) of it over the sea. This massive project includes an underwater tunnel, two artificial islands, and a series of bridges. Today, it takes about three hours to cross the Pearl River from Zhuhai or Macao to Hong Kong. The new link will cut this to 30 minutes when it opens in 2016.

The Fehmarn Belt Bridge

By 2018, cars and trains may be able to travel from Denmark to Germany across a bridge or under a tunnel. The decision is due to be made in 2013. If a bridge is chosen, the 12-mile-long (20 kilometer) link, called the Fehmarn Belt Bridge, will have a motorway and two railroad tracks. Today, the journey takes about an hour by ferry, but with a bridge, the journey time would be slashed to cut 15 minutes.

▼ *The Fehmarn Belt Bridge will have two decks, one above the other. One will be for road traffic and the other for trains.*

MEGA FACTS

A bridge across the Bering Strait would stand on 220 piers built in icy water and strengthened to protect them from the impact of icebergs.

Glossary

abutment
A massive block of stone or concrete that holds an arch in place.

anchorage
A massive concrete structure that holds a suspension bridge's cables firm.

bascule
A type of drawbridge that opens upwards, with the weight of the bridge balanced by a large weight called a counterweight.

beam
A long, thick slab of wood, metal, or concrete.

cantilever
A beam held up at one end only.

deck
The part of a bridge that people use to cross the bridge.

dredge
To dig up gravel or silt from under water.

footway
The part of a road bridge that is used by pedestrians.

gantry
A walkway or bridge-like structure, usually high off the ground, that links two parts of a building.

girder
A strong beam, usually made of steel, used in the construction of bridges and other large structures.

hanger
A vertical cable or chain that links the deck of a suspension bridge to the suspension cables. Hangers are also called suspenders.

hazard
Any risk or danger; something that may cause damage.

masonry
Any structure that is built from bricks, stone blocks, or concrete blocks.

pier
A support that holds up part of a bridge.

reinforced concrete
Concrete that has steel mesh or wire embedded in it to make it a lot stronger.

reservoir
An artificial lake used for storing water. A reservoir can be created by building a dam across a river.

rivet
A metal pin used to fasten together steel girders.

roadway
The part of a road bridge that is used by vehicles, such as cars, buses, and lorries.

strait
A sea channel between two pieces of land.

tunnel boring machine (TBM)
A giant vehicle with a rotating cutter head at the front that is used to dig a tunnel through the ground. A TBM is often custom-built to bore out a tunnel of a particular size.

viaduct
A bridge made from a line of arches or beams sitting on supports.

Top 5 longest bridges and tunnels

Bridges	Location	Completed
1. Lake Pontchartrain Causeway	USA	1956, 1969
2. Manchac Swamp Bridge	USA	1970
3. Yangcun Bridge	China	2007
4. Hangzhou Bay Bridge	China	2007
5. Runyang Bridge	China	2005

Tunnels	Location	Completed
1. Seikan Tunnel	Japan	1988
2. Channel Tunnel	England–France	1994
3. Lötschberg Base Tunnel	Switzerland	2007
4. Guadarrama Railway Tunnel	Spain	2007
5. Iwate-Ichinohe Tunnel	Japan	2002

Take it further

Is there a river near your home? What sort of bridge would you build across it?

Why do you think most of the world's longest bridges are suspension bridges? Why are they not arch bridges or beam bridges?

Why would soldiers break step (not march in time with each other) when they cross a bridge?

Think about why the longest bridges and tunnels are built. Would it be easier, quicker, and less expensive to build a road over or around a mountain than to build a tunnel?

Useful websites

www.longest-bridges.com
Log on to see pictures of and find out more about the world's longest bridges.

http://en.structurae.de/structures/stype
Links on bridges, viaducts, tunnels, and more.

Website information is correct at time of going to press. However, the publishers cannot accept liability for any information or links found on third-party websites.

Index